CHURCH PROGRAM MANAGEMENT

Effective Church Management

HENRY (HANK) LOYD COPELAND

authorHOUSE®

AuthorHouse™
1663 Liberty Drive
Bloomington, IN 47403
www.authorhouse.com
Phone: 1 (800) 839-8640

Published by AuthorHouse   09/28/2016

ISBN: 978-1-5246-4138-2 (sc)
ISBN: 978-1-5246-4137-5 (e)

Library of Congress Control Number: 2016916107

Print information available on the last page.

Dedication

This book is dedicated to those many church members who have unfortunately either decided to: a) not be a member of a church, or b) leave their current church and join another church. It is recognized that such dissatisfactions are deep rooted, frustrating, and can result in disappointment and anger. It is hoped that this book will contribute toward reducing some causes of these dissatisfactions.

This book also is dedicated first and foremost to his late wife with respect, gratitude, and affection:

Amy Elsie Suther Copeland
Wife, Mother, Friend, and Angel

This book also is dedicated to those twenty-five (25) families who were members of the Media Ministries team for several years.

Contents

Acknowledgement

The author acknowledges all those individuals who <u>unfortunately</u> sincerely and steadfastly stuck to the poor management 'business as usual' philosophy that destroyed (almost complete non-compliance with the Media Ministries Operating Plan) Media Ministries. If the author had not encountered this kind of poor management, this book would not have been written.

The author also acknowledges The Holy Spirit as providing 'peace that passes all understanding' to those who experience exposure to undesirable 'business as usual'.

Foreword

MESSAGE FROM THE HOLY SPIRIT: "...do everything in the name of the Lord Jesus..." Colossians 3:17.

It has been said that the greatest power in the world is the power to communicate with Almighty God. It is recommended that church leaders who read this book read it prayerfully and take each task to God in prayer for guidance in its identification and implementation.

The purpose of this book is to provide guidelines and motivate churches to more effectively perform the task of managing <u>programs</u> in the church. Management of the church, the BODY OF CHRIST on earth, is a very serious matter. As such, the church should be most interested in improving its efficiency and effectiveness. However, without knowing, many church Leaders continue to make no major changes in their management philosophy. In other words, 'business as usual' prevails.

Each church leader who reads this book must pay close attention to terms as defined in this book. It is recognized that churches have different organizational structures and identify different tasks and manage their church programs differently. This book presents a more classical management approach that is more consistent with secular business/management textbooks. This approach is widely used in business and is essential to success of the business. This approach can be a little foreign to those who have not used this approach. For example, the reader can be strongly inclined to say: "We don't do it this way." Yes, the reader must read the book as <u>a learning process</u> and understand what is being said even though it might be 'foreign' at first.

It is recognized that members of the church are from all ages and from different backgrounds. These differences result in the need for churches to adapt accordingly. However, all churches regardless of their outward operation must utilize the basic functions of management. For example, organizational components of the church must identify exactly what tasks they are to perform. This list of tasks comprises a plan. Experience shows that there are many advantages of preparing written plans. The same kinds of comments as stated here also apply to organizing, staffing, motivating, and controlling.

It is recognized that there are very small churches and very large churches. The guidelines in this book can be used by churches of all sizes. It is the management principles that are important. The organizational structure used in this book to communicate the management principals can easily be scaled down.

Churches that adopt guidelines contained in Appendix G can learn from each other. Also, one church that adopts these guidelines and places them in operation can be a model for many churches.

This book can be most useful for the following:

- Pastors (both Senior and Associate)
- Seminary Professors
- Seminary Students
- Other church related occupations, i.e. Minister of Music
- Lay Leaders
- Members of a church congregation

Pastors can use this book as guidelines in:
- setting up the church management structure,
- identifying church programs,
- managing church programs,
- educating church membership,
- preparing a body of members to become lay leaders, and
- developing and maintaining membership confidence in leadership.

Seminary professors can use this book as guidelines in preparing seminary students to contribute to churches both spiritually and managerially.

Lay leaders can use this book as guidelines to prepare themselves for leadership positions and support Pastors in performing their tasks.

Members of the congregation can use this book as guidelines to:

- better understand and appreciate the church
- identify leadership positions for which they have interest in filling,
- assess quality of church program management, and
- recommend church members for leadership positions.

Testimony

Media Ministries was founded by me during 2007; however, I did not know it. Over a period of seven years, the Holy Spirit guided me in small steps having me continually finance, design, build, staff, and operate Media Ministries. Appendix A presents the Operating Plan that documents this local and global ministry that I felt was desired by the Holy Spirit. It touched many people including the operating personnel as they became a happy team getting to work with each other and seeing what the Holy Spirit was building. It became a real joy to see the results of the Holy Spirit's guidance.

In 2015 the church assumed responsibility for Media Ministries; however, it was in name only. The 'business as usual' church leadership ignored the Operating Plan, and allowed Media Ministries to be destroyed (almost complete non-compliance with the Media Ministries Operating Plan). All of this invested time, talent, and money, as I saw it with my secular eyes, became of no value. Imagine the psychological impact of such a drastic change.

Initially, the feeling was deep hurt. Prayer in terms of "Thy will be done" was done in wonder. Why? Continual prayer led me to believe that the Holy Spirit did not want this kind of thing to happen and that He wants His church, The Body of Christ, managed much more efficiently and effective by getting rid of the business as usual philosophy. In my looking at the BIG picture, and trying to figure out where to go from here, I believe the Holy Spirit wants me to apply my management knowledge and experience to better help the universal church by writing "Church Program Management". This has a much broader scope than Media Ministries. This scope not only can affect one church, but it can improve the efficiency and effectiveness of all of God's churches.

Chapter 1
INTRODUCTION

MESSAGE TO CHURCH LEADERS
What are your preconceptions?
Do you have capability to change?
Are you open to changes?
Will your preconceptions stand in the way of improving
the efficiency and effectiveness of the church?

Instead of doubting everything that can be doubted, let us
rather doubt nothing until we are compelled to doubt.

MESSAGE FROM THE HOLY SPIRIT: "...do everything in the name of the Lord Jesus..." Colossians 3:17.

The entire purpose of this book is to be **positive**; to lift up or **build up** the church and not tear it down. This book must be read with a **positive attitude** looking for what might **improve** church **program** management performance. Improving implies change, and **change for the better**. Guidelines are provided to assist churches in improving performance. However, this book does use an example of a true major negative event caused by poor management to contrast or emphasize the need for change. This event is so negative that it can be falsely implied that its use is directed at one church and is cathartic for the author; neither is true. It is recognized that change is very difficult or near impossible for someone who has managed with virtually no change for years and sincerely feels there is no reason to change. In other words "it's not worth it". It is further recognized that: a) virtually all people are different for one reason or another, and as a result words have different meanings to different people, and b) churches are of different sizes, cultures, intellect, social status, and consist of all ages. All of this emphasizes the need for **training** to somehow get the audience to a similar **positive** thinking level. It is a fact that best communication takes place when the communication is between those who are alike. This is difficult to achieve especially when there are so many involved. Training must precede implementation. Implementation must be done slowly depending on the degree of training. Training must start with the most obvious to avoid creating mental blocks. *Now, if you are reading this book and have a negative thought, try the experiment of trying to discard that negative thought and turn a negative into a positive.*

The driver to managing church programs rests in the nature of the church or the personality of the church. Since the church is the body of Christ on earth, it is the secular and spiritual quality of the people in the church who identify and perform tasks that glorify God. This includes the entire leadership Board (defined in Chapter 2) plus all of the individual church members who are not on the leadership Board.

Even though it appears that making a list of tasks for a plan is secular in nature, the real motivator for identifying the tasks comes from within the individual people. Therefore, the personality of the church can be characterized by how the people act or their behavior. For example, some would concentrate on the appearance of the building first whereas some would put missions first.

Actions that characterize the personality or behavior of the church are many and can be seen in what it considers important, such as the following:

- Programs identified in its plans
- Attendance
- Stewardship
- Individual participation
- Treatment of visitors
- Treatment of guest participants

For example, how does the church respond when a member has not been seen attending church for a relatively extended time? Does the management structure include contacting the absent member and telling the member he/she is missed? Does the member just fade away? *Is the reason for absence so profound that the church can't handle it? If this is so, the church might have a deep rooted problem that needs attention.* Yes, it is possible that the absence can be from some cause that is relatively insignificant. This might be the way the 'business as usual' leader would respond independent of whether or not the absence was significant – just do nothing.

Many typical church members feel very comfortable in the church environment or they wouldn't be attending. They attend worship services, participate in a church sponsored activity like bible studies, choir, etc., have their friends, and appreciate the church in general. Some do not experience participation in the church governance, and those who do, get exposed to more or less the surface. Exposure below the surface reveals what the church is doing to grow the church and have a long term success in quantity of church members and spiritual impact on the community.

The one big excuse for acceptance of decline in number of church members is that 'church membership in many churches is on the decline'. There are many reasons for such decline; however, this decline should be a challenge to church leadership. In other words, leadership should DO SOMETHING ABOUT IT. The church should

3

not accept, in general, loss of membership, but should take advantage of anything that could grow the church. One thing that should be done is eliminate 'business as usual' since it is apparent that it is not working, and replace it with new 'church program management'.

FOUNDER/AUTHOR

'Here I am; send me."

The creation of Media Ministries took <u>several years</u>. As the scripture says, the Holy Spirit will give you no more to do than you are capable of handling. In this case, implementing the vision took: time, talent, and money. It is somewhat like founding a business. It progresses slowly in increments. The Author knows all of the details and has the best appreciation as to what is taking place and the difficulties encountered at every step. Even though a detailed Operating Plan was prepared and distributed to key people, and meetings were held with these key people, no one really grasped the total scope. No one really had an in-depth appreciation. In other words, no one <u>assumed responsibility</u> for reading the Operating Plan and assuring continuation of Media Ministries as defined in the Operating Plan. Therefore, leadership, <u>probably unintentionally</u>, allowed lack of compliance with the Operating Plan through neglect or 'business as usual'. Also, none of the congregation has read the Operating Plan, so it can think Media Ministries still exists even though it exists in name only. Decisions were made that destroyed Media Ministries and no one intervened. The term 'destruction' is used in lieu of any other term because the Author best understands what would be necessary to <u>recover</u> and <u>comply</u> with the Operating Plan. Chapter 2 recommends the following:

> Each Chair has to assume responsibility for <u>contributing to</u> the success not only of a Component but also for the entire Board by providing constructive criticism of each other Chair's plan and performance to plan.

4

BOARD & CONGREGATION

The Board including its Leader and Chairs <u>did not</u> "assume responsibility for contributing to the success of each Component of the Board". Not only was destruction allowed, but the Board and congregation still do not recognize that Media Ministries has been destroyed.

SUMMARY

Attempts were made to 'keep the Author 'satisfied', but these efforts were shallow 'business as usual'. It might seem that the Author is tearing down the church; however, to the contrary, this problem is so serious that it is necessary to 'tell it like it is' to aid in getting attention of leadership. Their ways must change. This is not 'tearing down' the church; it is a major attempt to 'build up' the church.

Chapters 2 through 7 provide recommended guidelines that will significantly improve church program management performance. Implementation of the guidelines will occur slowly and leadership must be **dedicated** and **persistent**. Leadership also will need to do a lot of **training.** Patience is required as well as continued FOLLOW THROUGH. Satisfactory results will be forthcoming.

In addition to the above, the Board, as defined in Chapter 2, must pass a POLICY STATEMENT (See Appendix G) motion that establishes these guidelines as permanent policy. This policy statement should include the fact that the moderator of the Board must use these guidelines in conducting <u>EACH</u> Board meeting.

Chapter 2

ORGANIZING

MESSAGE TO CHURCH LEADERS
What are your preconceptions?
Do you have capability to change?
Are you open to changes?
Will your preconceptions stand in the way of improving
the efficiency and effectiveness of the church?

Instead of doubting everything that can be doubted, let us
rather doubt nothing until we are compelled to doubt.

MESSAGE FROM THE HOLY SPIRIT: "...do everything in the name of the Lord Jesus..." Colossians 3:17.

The entire organization shown in Figure 1 – ORGANIZATIONAL STRUCTURE is referred to in this book as the "Leadership Board" and Board will be used for short. The Board in some churches is called Board of Deacons, and the Board in other churches is called Session. Other churches might have different names for the Board. The Board is composed of Components which are **top level** areas of responsibility. This terminology is not intended to represent any one or more religious traditions. This terminology is unique to this book. The Leader is in charge of the Board and a Chair is in charge of a Component. *The Board as a whole is not considered the Leader in this book. There is only one Leader who is the Leader of the Board and this Leader is responsible for the performance of each Chair. This Leader provides guidance and direction to each Chair.* The Leader's job description should include both management and spiritual. The Leader is a salaried professional ordained minister and has line authority over the Associate Leaders and the Chairs. Associate Leaders are salaried professionals who have expertise in one or more church discipline and a) perform their tasks within that discipline which is within the scope of one or more Components, and b) advise Chairs. The Chairs are volunteer members of the church and have authority over Associate Leaders. Each Chair should have its own task and its own budget to accomplish the task. For example, one Chair should <u>not</u> have control of all or part of the budget of another Chair. The Budgets & Accounting Chair should have final approval of the entire budget. Each Chair has to assume responsibility for <u>contributing</u> to the success not only of a Component but also for the success of the entire Board by providing guidance or constructive criticism of each other Chair's plan and performance to plan. **Appendix C** Example of Chair Critique- There will be cases where one or more tasks will be common to more than one Chair. An example of this task is shown in **Appendix B** – Hosting. Unless the Board assumes such responsibility, it is possible that any one or more of its

Components could perform poorly and even become totally ineffective.

Implementation of the guidelines in this book will occur slowly and leadership must be **dedicated** and **persistent**. Leadership also will need to do a lot of **training.** Patience is required as well as continued FOLLOW THROUGH. Satisfactory results will be forthcoming.

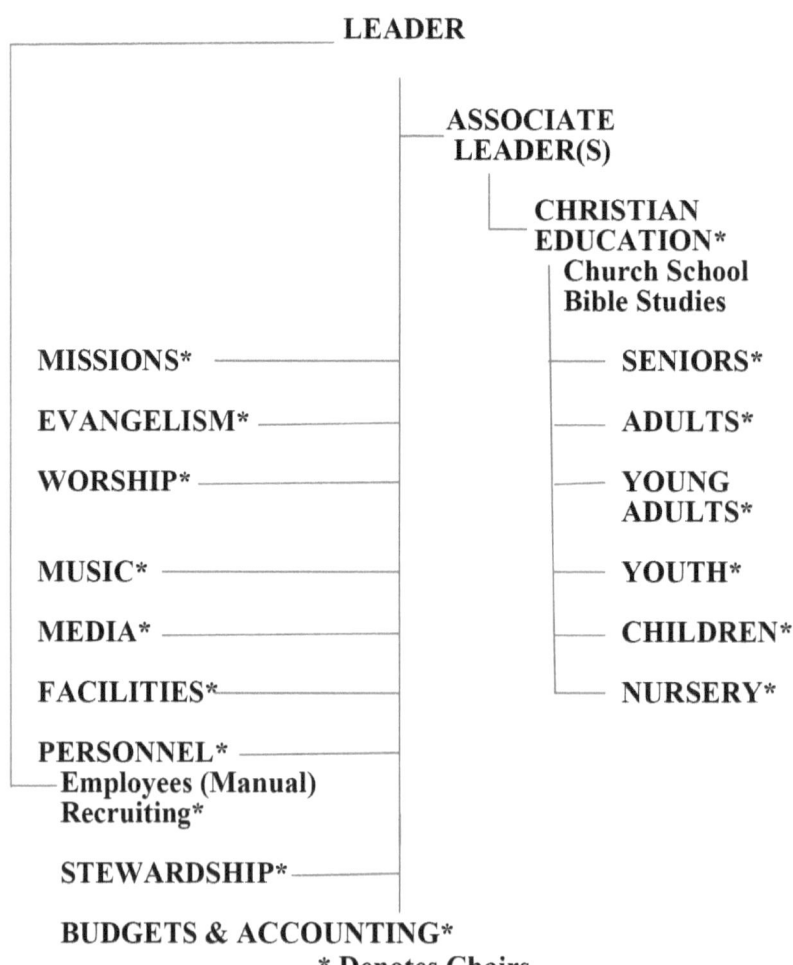

LEADER

ASSOCIATE LEADER(S)

CHRISTIAN EDUCATION*
Church School
Bible Studies

MISSIONS* — **SENIORS***

EVANGELISM* — **ADULTS***

WORSHIP* — **YOUNG ADULTS***

MUSIC* — **YOUTH***

MEDIA* — **CHILDREN***

FACILITIES* — **NURSERY***

PERSONNEL*
Employees (Manual)
Recruiting*

STEWARDSHIP*

BUDGETS & ACCOUNTING*
* Denotes Chairs

Figure 1 – ORGANIZATIONAL STRUCTURE

The type of structure in Figure 1 is common to many organizations. Some churches will have all of the noted components and some churches will have some differences and some churches will not have one or more of the components. In many cases the not-for-profit church is referred to as 'relational' and the for-profit businesses are referred to as 'hierarchical'. Both apply the basic functions of management included in business textbooks, namely,

- Planning
- Organizing
- Staffing
- Motivating
- Controlling

Planning comes before organizing in textbooks, based on the assumption that the organization currently does not exist, and organizing will occur as soon as there is a plan or something to organize. For purposes of this book it is assumed that a plan exists; even though it is extremely broad and not of sufficient detail to represent plans needed by each Chair. Therefore, in this book, Organizing precedes Planning.

As stated above, most if not all for-profit businesses manage using the hierarchical philosophy of communication when communicating between, for example, the Leader and Chairs. This philosophy is the most productive and mandatory for the organization to 'stay alive'. Why do churches use the relational technique? The answer is that the church is staffed with volunteers with exception of some paid employees, and **directing is considered too harsh for volunteers. This is a major fundamental misunderstanding as to how the hierarchical philosophy is used.** This misunderstanding can be largely due to having worked in only the church environment.

My experience while working in a hierarchical environment for over forty (40) years is that organizations using the hierarchical philosophy provide a lot of training in the areas of group centered leadership and communication. The organization sends its management personnel to weeks of concentrated training 'out of town' by professionals specializing in such and with paid expenses. The organization may even pay for all kinds of formal education including both Bachelors and Masters Degrees. The hierarchical managers work together with their employees to achieve the objectives. Each manager also is formally evaluated at regular intervals. A significant portion of the evaluation is employee relations. The good manager is not a dictator; the dictator is 'short lived'. The good manager is respected and promoted. Here again this is both true and contrary to the understanding of those in the church who use the relational philosophy.

Chapter 3
PLANNING

MESSAGE TO CHURCH LEADERS
What are your preconceptions?
Do you have capability to change?
Are you open to changes?
Will your preconceptions stand in the way of improving
the efficiency and effectiveness of the church?

Instead of doubting everything that can be doubted, let us
rather doubt nothing until we are compelled to doubt.

MESSAGE FROM THE HOLY SPIRIT: "…do everything in the name of the Lord Jesus…" Colossians 3:17.

The Leader should inform all Chairs that he/she is vitally interested in having each Chair prepare a plan for their organization, and that the Leader wants to help each Chair individually. This participation is proof to the Chairs that the Leader is most interested in each of them and wants each Chair to be a good manager and contribute to the successful performance of the church. This provides leadership development and development of the Chairs' spiritual gifts.

A plan is a list of objectives, and can contain descriptions of the objectives in both broad and detailed terms. It can include procedures as to how to achieve the objectives. It can include staffing requirements to achieve the objectives. In businesses there are tactical and strategic plans; tactical meaning near term and strategic meaning long term.

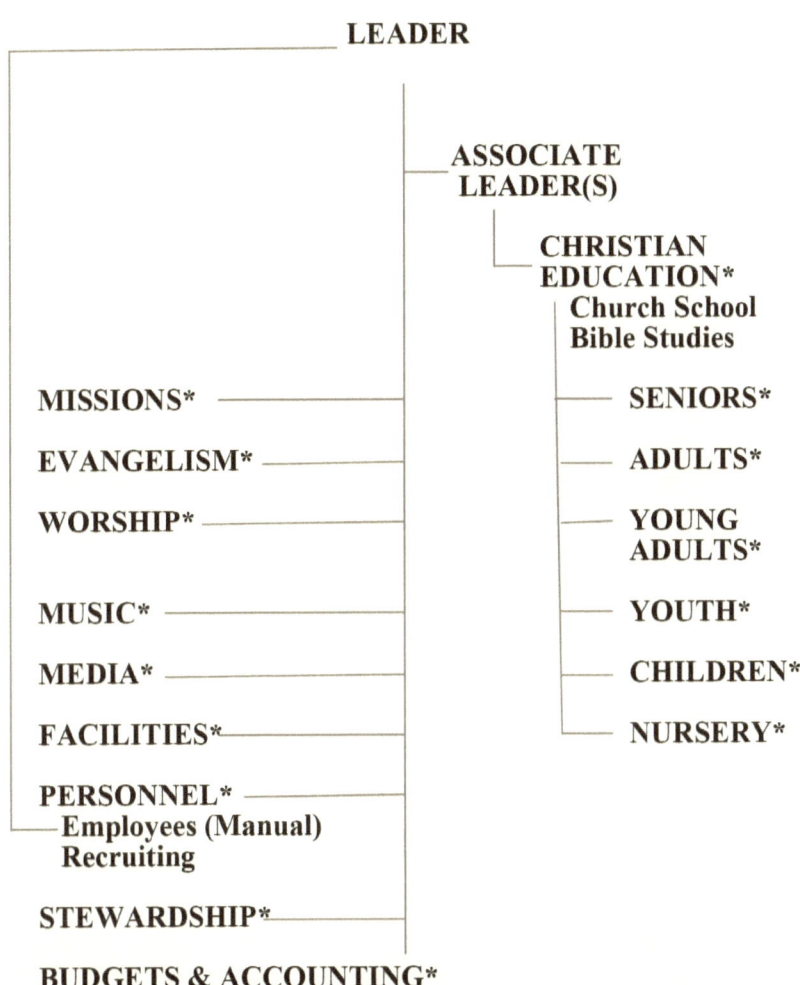

LEADER

ASSOCIATE
LEADER(S)

CHRISTIAN
EDUCATION*
Church School
Bible Studies

MISSIONS* ———————— —— SENIORS*

EVANGELISM* ————— —— ADULTS*

WORSHIP* ————————— —— YOUNG
ADULTS*

MUSIC* ———————————— —— YOUTH*

MEDIA* ———————————— —— CHILDREN*

FACILITIES*——————— —— NURSERY*

PERSONNEL* ——————
—— Employees (Manual)
Recruiting

STEWARDSHIP*——————

BUDGETS & ACCOUNTING*

• Denotes Chairs

Figure 1 – ORGANIZATIONAL STRUCTURE

It appears obvious that every church should have and most likely does have plans. However, because of the nature of the relational management philosophy and business as usual used by Leaders in the church, the plan is not used as it should be used. Leaders in the church have different experiences from those who have successfully used the hierarchical management philosophy. Most Leaders in the church have no experience in managing an organization firmly grounded in getting tasks accomplished thru use of <u>in-depth</u> basic management functions. There is a sense that virtually no direction should be provided. There is a lack of understanding of the meaning of direction. It appears to leadership in the church that 'direction' comes from a dictator type of personality which should not be used when the Board consists of mostly volunteers. This understanding can so permeate the organization that:

- A plan for each Chair does not exist.
- There is no adequate documentation of previous performance.
- There is no transition of leadership because little to no documentation exists.
- Chairs are appointed as Chairs without properly matching capability to task.
- Chairs are assigned poorly defined tasks for which it is assumed they will assume responsibility.
- Chairs vary in capability from capable to very little capability.
- Little to no direction is provided to Chairs.
- Lack of direction produces minimal results.
- Lack of **Leader** involvement in Chair task performance results in lack of in-depth knowledge of the status of the task and possible knowledge of the task itself.
- Chairs have no budgets, and as a result are not involved in performing to budget or forecasting to budget.

When there is no plan, it is very common in the church that every year, without question, newly recruited Chairs say: "What am I supposed to do; am I supposed to reinvent the wheel; there is no plan for my 'component' or committee; what was done during the previous year(s); what am I to do now?" Yes, this is sad especially when only a mission statement exists for the Chairs. Without an operating plan, there is little to no effective transition.

CAUTION – It is not enough to have a plan without some detail as to how to implement the plan. For example, the following are good objectives, but detail must exist as to how to achieve the objectives:

- Experience Jesus
- Strengthen Christ's Church
- Journey Into Deeper Faith
- Transform Our World

Without either detail or plan and without follow up, it is doubtful that the good objectives will ever be achieved.

A plan is a 'working' document. It is prepared for several reasons, some of which are it:

- Communicates to others that the Board not only is in name only, but the Board is well managed
- Organizes the Chair's thoughts
- Identifies tasks that can be assigned to the Chair's staff
- The Chair's staff know what they are to do
- Is a reference for reporting
- Tells others what the Chair plans to do
- Provides others with the opportunity to contribute to its content
- Is a major aid in transitioning the task to others
- Is an aid in training Chairs to manage

Preparing a plan does require <u>thought</u>, and it does require someone to <u>write</u>. A Chair without proper management experience can say: "We really don't need this." This is a 'business as usual do nothing attitude', and is the 'easy way out', and limits the entire church contribution, and especially individual contribution and appreciation of the church. All that needs to be done is to <u>ask</u> someone, even without experience, to prepare a plan and provide as much help as practical. **Appendix D – Youth Operating Plan** is a very rough example of tasks that might be included in a "Youth Operating Plan".

With assistance from the Leader, one Chair who has never prepared a plan can start preparation of a plan that consists of possibly very few tasks. Then, the needed staff is identified; they are recruited; the recruited personnel begin to see results; an esprit de corps develops; and the Chair begins to appreciate the results.

The Chair might even add tasks to the plan. The almost non-existent organization grows. The entire church begins to see and appreciate the results and the personality of the church changes for the better especially when each of the Chairs does the same. This does require dedicated and capable leadership including especially follow through.

Not only will the leadership be motivated, but the entire congregation would be motivated when leadership is 'open' and communicates fully with the congregation. The congregation could communicate its desires for including items based on their personal experiences at work or in a previous church. However, the atmosphere must be such to encourage such participation. Unfortunately, without this encouragement, capable church members are relegated to just attending Worship Services and maybe a Bible Study, and then go home. This is a massive loss in contribution.

BUDGET

Budget is part of the plan. The Leader and each Chair should have its own task and its own budget to accomplish the task. For example, one Chair should not have control of all or part of the budget of another Chair. The Budgets & Accounting Chair should have final approval of the entire budget and authority to make revisions to the budget as required. Plans must be the basis of allocating budgets and as such, performance to budget is the task of each Chair. Since the task of some Chairs will be performed entirely by volunteers, there is no need for a budget for all Chairs. There should be a one-to-one relationship between the task(s) to be performed and the budgets for the task(s) to be performed. In turn, the Chair could provide budget forecasts.

Chapter 4
STAFFING

MESSAGE TO CHURCH LEADERS
What are your preconceptions?
Do you have capability to change?
Are you open to changes?
Will your preconceptions stand in the way of improving
the efficiency and effectiveness of the church?

Instead of doubting everything that can be doubted, let us
rather doubt nothing until we are compelled to doubt

MESSAGE FROM THE HOLY SPIRIT: "...do everything in the name of the Lord Jesus..." Colossians 3:17.

Staffing requirements are determined by the structure of the organization and the plans prepared by the Chairs. The structure identifies the Leader, Associate Leaders, and the Chairs, and the Chairs' prepare plans that identify their personnel requirements to staff their plans. In all cases, job descriptions describe the tasks to be accomplished.

Recruiting is <u>one</u> of the most important tasks to be performed. Advertising should be used; however, knowledge of the congregation and the 'personal touch' should be emphasized.

Recruiting requires a 'personal touch'. Recruiting is a <u>continual</u> task needed to replace attrition.

The objective of recruiting volunteers is to identify and get a commitment from a prospective person or recruit to staff a job that this person can perform successfully. This requires the recruiter to match the person's capability with the job description. Some jobs would require stronger spiritual gifts than others. The job description can be very brief; it does <u>not</u> have to be complex.

An approach to recruiting that has been successful includes the following:

- Establish a <u>permanent</u> Recruiting Committee that is active year around to perform all recruiting requirements
- Prepare a recruiting plan
- Prepare a job description for the Recruiting Committee
- Prepare the Leader's job description and job descriptions of each Chair
- Board to submit both the plans and job descriptions from each Chair to the Recruiting Committee
- Proceed to staff each Chair's organization in coordination with each Chair

The following is an example of how many churches recruit. This is how <u>not</u> to recruit.....

EXAMPLE – Most recruiting committees are temporary in nature, and disbanded after recruiting either or both the Leader and Chairs. The Chairs, when recruited, are not aware of the task they are to perform; the Leader assigns each recruit to a task after they are recruited. The recruiting committees receive recommendations and conduct brief interviews. In most cases a new prospect passes the interview based on personality and desire to serve. There is no <u>written</u> job description of the job to which they ultimately are assigned, and there is no <u>written</u> plan for the task to be accomplished. Also, there is little to no <u>written</u> information about what was previously accomplished. These new leaders are placed in individual leadership positions without knowing what is to be done. In some cases there is an overall understanding based on the title of the position and possibly an overall paragraph describing his/her organization. This newly recruited person must somehow gather enough knowledge to begin doing 'something' that is considered to be the task.

It should be noted that once the organizational structure is in place, and plans are prepared and each Chair has staffed their component, the organization, the plans, and the staffing can remain in place almost indefinitely. Plans most likely will be revised periodically and staff attrition will require some periodic recruiting.

Chapter 5

MOTIVATING & CONTROLLING

MESSAGE TO CHURCH LEADERS
What are your preconceptions?
Do you have capability to change?
Are you open to changes?
Will your preconceptions stand in the way of improving
the efficiency and effectiveness of the church?

Instead of doubting everything that can be doubted, let us
rather doubt nothing until we are compelled to doubt.

MESSAGE FROM THE HOLY SPIRIT: "...do everything in the name of the Lord Jesus..." Colossians 3:17.

The Leader's 'human touch' is so important in motivating and controlling. The Leader must not be a dictator. The Leader must be a 'friend'. The Leader should inform all Chairs that he/she is vitally interested in working with each Chair individually. A by-product of this working together is that both the Leader and Chair learn, and as a result the congregation is educated and feels that they are involved and can contribute. The entire church grows.

The atmosphere during each Board meeting and each Leader meeting with each Chair must be mutual respect between everyone on the Board and especially mutual respect between the Leader and each Chair. There should be no embarrassment, and everyone should have the attitude of wanting to help each other.

LEADER MODERATES BOARD

The routine Board agenda should include for each Chair:
- Policy statement (See Chapter 2)
- Status of plan preparation
- Identification of each task included in the plan
- Identification of current active and potentially active tasks
- Staffing status including job description of Chair and job description of staff
- Current task activity status
- Budget status
- Request for Chair critiques, suggestions, and evaluations; recommended additions, deletions, and modifications

There is no place for trying to make the meeting 'short'. This does not imply that inefficiency is acceptable. The emphasis should be on 'getting the job done'. The Leader and Chairs should have the desire to produce the best plans feasible, and implement these plans effectively.

LEADER MEETING WITH CHAIR

The routine agenda should include essentially the same elements as included in the Board meeting:

- Status of plan preparation
- Identification of each task included in the plan
- Identification of current active and potentially active tasks
- Staffing status including job description of Chair and job description of staff
- Current task activity status
- Budget status
- Request for Chair critiques; recommended additions, deletions, and modifications

CAUTION – FOLLOW THROUGH!!

Implementation of the organizational structure included in Chapter 2 and the meeting approach noted above can take a relatively long time for everyone to feel comfortable, so patience is required as well as continued FOLLOW THROUGH. Satisfactory results will be forthcoming.

BUSINESS AS USUAL VS IN-DEPTH USE OF BASIC FUNCTIONS OF MANAGEMENT

Many churches use the 'business as usual' management philosophy with extremely limited applications of the basic functions of management. This limited use of these functions produces limited results, and in some cases no results. These functions are in business textbooks to provide managers the way to successfully achieve high performance yielding much desired results. Churches should avoid the 'business as usual' philosophy especially when there are proven management philosophies that produce high performance with much better results.

Leaders who use the 'business as usual' concept, continue down the same path as always and are quite satisfied with current performance, and see no reason to change. The 'business as usual' management philosophy provides no improvement. Their 'minds are made up' and little interest exists in improvement. See **Appendix E** – Operating Plan Proposal that was rejected. The mind must be honestly open and seek new ideas. **'Business as usual' has been used for years and getting leadership to change even for improvement is very difficult and,**

unfortunately, sometimes impossible. Basic business functions, when properly understood and applied while working together provide a synergistic result that produces the end result which is the objective of effectively managing programs in the church.

RELATIONAL MANAGEMENT PHILOSOPHY

The church ~~is~~ can be referred to as a 'relational' organization because it dominantly consists of volunteers in contrast to paid personnel. To some, this implies providing very little detailed Leader involvement resulting in providing virtually no direction. Providing direction as in the hierarchical organization is considered dictatorial in nature by 'relational' leaders. Hierarchical management really is relational with one exception, and that is the Leader has the unchallenged authority to make decisions and provide direction. This is not considered dictatorial. It is considered 'good business practice'. Making decisions, and providing direction, must be done in an acceptable manner to achieve desired results. There is no place for a dictator, and **the dictator will have difficulty surviving.**

BUSINESS AS USUAL RESPONSE TO CHANGE

The 'business as usual' management philosophy provides no improvement. Their 'minds are made up' and little interest exists in improvement. The mind must be <u>honestly</u> open and seek new ideas.

When attempts are being made to get the "business as usual" leader to implement change, there can appear that progress to change is being made; however, you will not know until changes are really made.

The following are some of the characteristics most likely present:
- Inherently 'business as usual' – no change
- Perceived barriers – no available funds; can't afford it; no change in overall budget structure
- Mutual respect – perceived barriers over shadow mutual respect
- Sincerity – questionable
- Tolerance – tolerance without change; delay tactics
- Desire to understand new ideas – questionable
- Capability to understand new ideas – questionable

Chapter 6
TRAINING

MESSAGE TO CHURCH LEADERS
What are your preconceptions?
Do you have capability to change?
Are you open to changes?
Will your preconceptions stand in the way of improving
the efficiency and effectiveness of the church?

Instead of doubting everything that can be doubted, let us
rather doubt nothing until we are compelled to doubt.

MESSAGE FROM THE HOLY SPIRIT: "…do everything in the name of the Lord Jesus…" Colossians 3:17.

Leadership training sessions should be conducted by the Recruiting Committee in two stages:

- Current Board
- Congregation

Each new Board should be trained and congregation training should be continued throughout the year.

It is recognized that many church members consider such training sessions boring and uninteresting. The Recruiting Committee must recognize this and 'market' this training. This will require a lot of thought and preparation to create interest. Personal contacts with invitations could be used.

Many congregation members really are ~~not~~ either not familiar with the existing management philosophy or really don't care. They know the organization and some job titles, but know little of the details. Therefore, the congregation should have the opportunity to learn, and many will attend meetings focused on training personnel to understand the:

- Church's management concept,
- Job descriptions, and
- Opportunities to serve

A PowerPoint presentation should be prepared covering the above, and opportunities should be provided for members of the congregation to attend. Refer to **Appendix F** – Training. These training sessions also should be used to have congregation members express their interest in one or more opportunities to serve.

Chapter 7

SUMMARY

MESSAGE TO CHURCH LEADERS
What are your preconceptions?
Do you have capability to change?
Are you open to changes?
Will your preconceptions stand in the way of improving
the efficiency and effectiveness of the church?

Instead of doubting everything that can be doubted, let us
rather doubt nothing until we are compelled to doubt.

MESSAGE FROM THE HOLY SPIRIT: "...do everything in the name of the Lord Jesus..." Colossians 3:17.

This book can be quite useful for the following:
- Pastors (both Senior and Associate)
- Seminary Professors
- Seminary Students
- Other church related occupations
- Lay Leaders

'Business as usual' provides no improvement. 'Minds are made up' and little interest exists in improvement. This book can be quite useful for 'business as usual' leaders if, and only if, they are receptive to change including major changes.

Problems discussed in this book indicate that there are churches that just 'chug' along without any thought of improvement and actually reject means of improvement. There is considerable room for improvement, and guidelines in this book, when applied, can provide it.

Many typical church members feel very comfortable in the church environment. They attend worship services, participate in a church sponsored activity like bible studies, choir, etc., have their friends, and appreciate the church in general. Some do not experience participation in the church governance, and those who do get exposed to more or less the surface. Exposure below the surface reveals what the church is doing to grow the church and have a long term success in membership and the spiritual impact on the community.

'Business as usual' should be eliminated since it is apparent that it is not working, and replace it with new 'church program management'. 'Business as usual' cannot only detrimentally contribute to quantity of membership decline, but also can allow destruction of successful portions of the church such as Media Ministries. Also, the Leader and Chairs should recognize the positive significance of providing direction and voluntarily provide 'direction' to each other for mutual benefit.

Churches that adopt guidelines contained in this book can learn from each other. Involvement, at its best, yields ownership. Ownership reflects commitment. Also, one church that adopts these guidelines and places them in operation can be a model for many churches.

MEDIA MINISTRIES OPERATING PLAN

MESSAGE TO CHURCH LEADERS
What are your preconceptions?
Do you have capability to change?
Are you open to changes?
Will your preconceptions stand in the way of improving
the efficiency and effectiveness of the church?

Instead of doubting everything that can be doubted, let us
rather doubt nothing until we are compelled to doubt.

NOTE: Portions of this plan have been redacted to avoid identifying the specific church at which this plan was used. The redacted book location is identified by brackets, thusly, [ ].

PURPOSE – This plan is used to document and manage operation of Media Ministries. This plan is available to anyone who is interested in: a) understanding the organization, b) evaluating performance, and c) identifying potential improvements.

MISSION: The mission is to multiply the number of individuals, both local and global, who hear sermons, participate in Bible study, pursue knowledge of church activities, and pursue a personal relationship with Jesus Christ. This mission is achieved by utilization of sound, light, projection, and video recordings of Worship Services and Bible Studies to capture videos which are uploaded to vimeo.com for viewing (playing).

STATISTICS: Vimeo.com provided the following statistics covering five and one half years beginning March 2009 and ending October 1, 2014:

Total Plays	11,628
Plays per Month	174
Plays per Week	43

This is equivalent to a Bible Study class running 52 weeks per year for five (5) years with 43 attending every week.

INTRODUCTION –The Recording Ministry was established in memory of [] in 2007 and is privately financed. The original missions were to video record Worship Services and create DVDs for those who could not attend Worship Services for various reasons. At that time the name, Recording Ministry, was appropriate. Since then the Recording Ministry has significantly expanded its assumption of responsibility to include not only Video Recording and DVD creation, duplication, and distribution, but also:

- Sound
- Theatrical Lighting
- Video Recording, Processing, and Original Creation
- Computer Projection-Video & Sound
- Assisted Listening
- Still Photography

- DVD Cover Design, Duplication & Distribution
- Audio/Video Cart
- Support of Church Activities
- Video Broadcasting-Real Time Streaming Video (TBD)

Therefore, the name, Recording Ministry, was changed to Media Ministries; to be better representative.

Media Ministries reports to [ ].

Media Ministries facilities include: [ ].

MISSION – Enhance Worship Services and Pastor's Bible Study. Multiply the number of individuals, both local and global, who hear/ view sermons, participate in Bible study, pursue knowledge of church activities, and pursue a personal relationship with Jesus Christ. Support Café Worship as required. Support various church organizations, functions at the church, and enable use of audio and video.

CREDIT – Our life is the life of Christ, mediated in us by the indwelling Holy Spirit. The more constant our communication with the indwelling Christ, the better we are pruned and the more fruit we are able to produce. Any accomplishments of ours are due to Christ, not to our own effort. Colossians 3:17 – [17] And whatever you do, whether in word or deed, do it all in the name of the Lord Jesus, giving thanks to God the Father through him.

Remember, you are working for God, not individuals.

STAFFING – The following staffing is provided on a weekly basis:
- 1 ea. – Sanctuary preparation for events
- 1 ea. – Video camera recording (One Worship Service)
- 1 ea. – Sound/mixer operation (Two Worship Services)
- 1 ea. – Projection (Two Worship Services)
- 1 ea. – Lighting control (Two Worship Services)
- 1 ea. – Video download from camera recording to computer, then upload to vimeo.com
- 1 ea. – Video editing of Worship Service video, then upload to vimeo.com
- 2 ea. – Daybreak Bible Study (video recording, mixer operation, projection)
- 1 ea. – Personnel Assignments (Sound/mixer, Projection, Lighting, Camera operation)

Staffing also is provided for special events such as the following including rehearsals:

- Piano Recital
- Organ Recital
- Children's Choir Musical
- Children's Christmas Eve Program
- Vacation Bible School
- [ ] Summer Concert
- Christmas Concert
- Others

Staffing also is provided during the week to support requests from the church staff and others within the church.

TECHNICAL TASKS – Including:

- Assure appropriate setup of sound in the Sanctuary and Chapel for events.
- Maintain the technical portion of the Media Ministries Manual.
- Interface, when necessary, with [ ].
  - Perform Reverberation Time tests in the Sanctuary when deemed necessary
  - Calibrate/adjust Digital Signal Processor when deemed necessary
- Battery management; assure charged batteries are available as needed and installed in appropriate equipment including both the wireless mics used in the Sanctuary and the Assisted Listening receivers.
- Video recording is performed using a Sony Solid-State Memory Camcorder PMW-EX-1 mounted on a Manfrotto fluid mount tripod.
- Running sound is performed by use of inputs from microphones and media playback devices to Yamaha L9-32 Digital Mixer.
- Projection is accomplished by laptop computer input to two Mitsubishi DLP XD8100U projectors and one Panasonic PT-VX400NT projector – two for the Congregation and one for the Chancel.

- Align the two images projected from the Mitsubishi projectors when necessary.
- Lighting control of twelve theatrical lights is performed using a laptop computer with LightFactory software controlling lights via DMX communication protocol involving four Chauvet PRO-6 Dimmer Relay Racks
- Video processing is performed using Sony Vegas Pro 12 software installed on three desktop computers linked together on one Network Drive.
- DVDs are duplicated using a Sony Duplicator which duplicates seven disks 'simultaneously'.
- DVD covers are designed and printed directly on the disk using Epson Print CD software.
- DVDs are distributed weekly to those unable to attend Worship Services.
- Still photography produces photos edited with Photoshop software for documentation and communication purposes.
- Prepare PowerPoint presentations.
- Perform equipment and software maintenance and upgrade.
- Provide training for personnel.
- Provide support to the Café Worship Service.

[ ]

ADMINSTRATIVE TASKS – Administrative tasks include:
- Prepare and maintain current the Administration portion of the Media Ministries Manual.
- Schedule and assign personnel weekly to operate camera, mixer, computer for projection, and lighting control computer for each event.
- Distribute DVDs.
- Provide safe storage of master disks for backup and duplication.
- Recruit and train personnel.
- Provide maintenance for computers and peripherals
- Procure computer and camera equipment and office supplies.
- Report activities to Business Administrator.

- Maintain current the Assisted Listening Ear Bud assignment 'board'.
- Prepare articles for Worship Service Bulletin and Spire.
- Analyze Vimeo media statistics and produce reports.
- Provide physical storage with ready access for video sound, and lighting equipment.
- Procure Vimeo storage periodically as additional storage is needed.
- Provide audio/video cart for church personnel usage

[ ]

GUIDELINES FOR RECRUITING
- Capability/expertise – Continue to observe congregation including New Member Biographies and identify those who have backgrounds suitable/adaptable to performing Media Ministries' tasks. Interview these personnel during a one-on-one meeting in which all aspects of Media Ministries are discussed and viewed. Ask the interviewee his/her areas of interest. Proceed accordingly.
- Availability – Get a commitment that 'feels' natural and not pressured.
- Devotion to task – "Measure" the interviewee's capability-availability-depth of interest. The result must be of mutual interest.
- Degree of interest in the mission of the ministry
- Spouse support is vital; communicate this point and express appreciation for the support.
- One of the major results of staffing Media Ministries is a 'bonding' among staff.

GUIDELINES FOR PERFORMANCE IMPROVEMENT
Two major aspects of performing a task: 1) perform the task well, and 2) allocate time and 'brain power' to identify how performance of the task can be improved.
- Quality – Don't squeeze yourself on memory and speed; result can be marginal performance; tactfully critique performance; provide help.

- Versatility – Some software is more simple and easier to use than the more complex; don't sacrifice capability for simplicity. The more complex becomes easier to use as the learning process continues.
- Media Ministries gets high visibility; mistakes are inevitable.
- Many are prepared to criticize and few are prepared to compliment; recognize that it is inevitable that you will be criticized; _remember you are working for God, not individuals._

Appendix B
HOSTING GUIDELINES

MESSAGE TO CHURCH LEADERS
What are your preconceptions?
Do you have capability to change?
Are you open to changes?
Will your preconceptions stand in the way of improving
the efficiency and effectiveness of the church?

Instead of doubting everything that can be doubted, let us
rather doubt nothing until we are compelled to doubt.

NOTE: Portions of these guidelines have been redacted to avoid identifying the specific church at which this plan was used. The redacted book location is identified by brackets, thusly, [].

This is a very rough draft. [] have experienced guests arriving at the church having no contact; just floating around. [] have experienced 'last minute' need for a host.

At least three areas have guests/visitors to the church of various types and should host these guests. These areas include:

➢ Pastor(s)
➢ Mission Component
➢ Worship and Music Component

The Pastor has guests/visitors to the church that fall into two categories: a) more personal guests he/she prefers hosting, and b) guests he/she would expect the Worship Component host.

Guests from, for example, the [ ] should be hosted by the Mission Component. Guest musicians and guest choirs, both children and adults, for example, should be hosted by the Music Component. Guests of Pastor(s) not hosted by Pastor(s) should be hosted by the Worship Component. Hosting is a very important task and can at times be very involved.

CASE FOR MISSION COMPONENT (See Chapter 2 Organization Structure)

Example No. 1: Guest arriving via airline, has no transportation, and needs lodging.

➢ Identify Host and get commitment that he/she will be responsible for the guest from arrival to departure. In case the committee chair cannot perform the task of the host, it is the responsibility of this chair to identify a host within his/her committee and 'train' the 'substitute' in details such as those noted below. In some cases it might be necessary for the chair to cancel previous personal plans and perform the task of host.
➢ Name of Host
➢ Name of Guest
➢ Airline
➢ Arrival time
➢ Departure time

- ➢ Meet guest at airport
- ➢ Transport guest during entire visit
- ➢ Accommodate any special needs of the guest, and there can be one or more.
- ➢ Provide lodging (first night)
- ➢ Provide breakfast
- ➢ Transport guest to church
- ➢ Introduce guest to many members
- ➢ Arrange for guest to meet with group(s)
- ➢ Make reservations for lunch
- ➢ Invite <u>specific members</u>, not the entire church, to attend luncheon
- ➢ Attend luncheon and pay guests tab
- ➢ Tour guest over the city to previously planned sites
- ➢ Provide a resting place like for the remainder of the afternoon in the Host's home
- ➢ Take guest to dinner
- ➢ Provide lodging (last night)
- ➢ Take guest to airport for departure
- ➢ Others not included above

In case the Host is assisted by one or more individuals, all individuals involved need to know the specific hour when and where the exchange is to take place, not just in the morning or afternoon.

CASE FOR MUSIC COMPONENT (See Chapter 2 Organization Structure)

<u>Example No. 2</u>:

Two groups are performing and **we need a single host to be in charge of this**, are: 1) [], and 2) []. These groups already have accommodations. Needs exist for guides here on church campus doing the following:

- ➢ Check singers in and tell them where to go (pass out little maps of our campus)
- ➢ Attend to needs of directors: last minute things. All set-up needs should be prepared in advance: tables, chairs, computer needs, projectors, sound, heat, music stands, water, coffee, tissues, pencils, welcome signs or specific directional sign,

etc. Someone should be responsible for double checking all of that before anyone arrives.

➢ Managing the schedule and facilitating movement of groups to their assigned rooms, etc. during this festival, there are three to four groups who rehearse at the same time at various locations and then need to move to rehearse together with other groups - we are talking about moving 150-200 children all at once! We should have a guide assigned to each group who knows the campus and can assist with any needs that arise for that group. Children can get sick, have to use the bathroom, pass out, start crying and feeling homesick, etc. during rehearsal.

This particular event needs a team of people with **<u>one person in charge</u>**, being the host, to manage this task so everything goes smoothly. [] is meeting with the event organizers on [], and it would be most desirable for this host attend this meeting with me.

Appendix C
EXAMPLE OF CHAIR CRITIQUE

MESSAGE TO CHURCH LEADERS
What are your preconceptions?
Do you have capability to change?
Are you open to changes?
Will your preconceptions stand in the way of improving
the efficiency and effectiveness of the church?

Instead of doubting everything that can be doubted, let us
rather doubt nothing until we are compelled to doubt.

The Chair has done a very good job; however, there are some recommended additions, deletions, and changes to the Chair's plan.

It is recommended that the following be added:

1.
2.
3.
Etc.

It is recommended that the following be deleted:

1.
2.
3.
Etc.

It is recommended that the following be changed:

1.
2.
3.
Etc.

It is recommended that the following tasks be moved from this Chair to another Chair.

The staffing will need to be revised to incorporate the above.

YOUTH OPERATING PLAN EXAMPLE

MESSAGE TO CHURCH LEADERS
What are your preconceptions?
Do you have capability to change?
Are you open to changes?
Will your preconceptions stand in the way of improving
the efficiency and effectiveness of the church?

Instead of doubting everything that can be doubted, let us
rather doubt nothing until we are compelled to doubt.

NOTE: This plan is only a rough guide. Initial preparation can start with much less contend and be improved as progress is made. Staffing is a prime consideration.

PURPOSE

The purpose of this plan is to: communicate with both Leadership and the congregation.

Some of the items that could be included in the plan are:
1. Christian education
2. Spiritual fellowship
3. Family Christian growth
4. Entertainment
5. Worship opportunities
6. Outreach to non-churched youth and their families;
7. Parent development and adult counselors and sponsors.
8. Development of a young ministry leadership team;
9. Opportunities for Youth to get exposure and participate in as many church adult Component activities as practical.

DATABASE

Build and maintain a database to include the following:
- Youth in church-member households
- Youth in church non-member households
- Records of:
    - ✓ Attendance
    - ✓ Event participation
    - ✓ Individual contacts to encourage Youth in church non-member households to become active in the Youth ministry
- Prepare reports of the above

1. CHRISTIAN EDUCATION

Provide Christian education using a Christian Education curriculum in classroom environment for K-7 through K-12 during the public school year. An example of the curriculum is as follows:
[Include example]

2. SPIRITUAL FELLOWSHIP

- Provide activities on campus and off campus.
- Integrate Youth into as many adult organizations as practical (A parent could/should accompany the youth.)

3. CHRISTIAN ENTERTAINMENT

Provide Christian entertainment in a variety of forms on church campus and off-site.
[Expand to include details.]

4. FAMILY GROWTH

Integrate Youth into as many adult organizations as practical (Encourage parent(s) to accompany the youth.)
[Expand to include details]

5. WORSHIP

Provide Youth Worship Services following a specific agenda each Sunday following Christian Education classes. The agenda should include elements of Service provided in the Main Sanctuary.
[Expand to include details]

6. OUTREACH TO NON-CHURCHED YOUTH AND THEIR FAMILIES

Use the database noted under Christian Education above.
[Expand to include details]

7. MISSION OUTREACH

[Expand to include details]

8. PARENT AND ADULD COUNSELORS AND SPONSORS

[Expand to include details]

9. YOUNG MINISTRY LEADERSHIP TEAM

[Expand to include details]

10. COMMITMENT TO CHRISTIAN SERVICE

[Expand to include details]

11. PARTICIPATION IN EACH LEDERSHIP COMPONENT ACTIVITY

[Expand to include details]

12. PARTICIPATION IN PREPARATION OF DATA FOR INCLUSION ON CHURCH WEBSITE

[Expand to include details]

Appendix E

OPERATING PLAN – PROPOSAL TO LEADERSHIP

MESSAGE TO CHURCH LEADERS
What are your preconceptions?
Do you have capability to change?
Are you open to changes?
Will your preconceptions stand in the way of improving
the efficiency and effectiveness of the church?

Instead of doubting everything that can be doubted, let us
rather doubt nothing until we are compelled to doubt.

NOTE: This was a presentation to Leadership resulting in a lack of acceptance. The proposal just 'died'. The term 'committee' is used here since the church for which this was presented uses the term committee instead of component used in this book.

PURPOSE
OF
OPERATING PLAN

Provide basis for:
- **More complete definition of task to be performed**
- **Greater participation by Leaders in Committee Operation**
- **Improved communication with:**
  - ✓ **Committees**
  - ✓ **Congregation**
- **Improved Committee performance**
- **Specific constructive criticism**
- **New Leader orientation**
- **Continuity**
- **Mission re-evaluation**

CURRENT SITUATION
Leadership relative to Committees

Leadership Participation
- Brief monthly reports/statements

Leadership communication
- Listen to monthly reports/statements
- Virtually no feedback to committees

Leadership contribution to performance
- Relatively none

Leadership constructive criticism
- Relatively none

Committee performance improvement
- Little incentive

New Leader orientation
- None in most cases

Continuity
- Word of mouth
- Dependent on characteristics of assigned Leader

Re-evaluate mission
- None

RESULT

Entire operation is STATUS QUO with some exceptions:
- Routine matters
- Special occasions
- Problems encountered

NO FIX
OR
FIX

- Continue status quo
- Assume Leadership responsibility and fix the problem

EXPECTATIONS

Each Chair read/study submitted Operating Plan

Recommend additions/deletions/revisions in form of:
- Written book and/or
- Mark-up of Operating Plan

Chairs:
- Incorporate additions/deletions/revisions as deemed necessary
- Provide feedback to source of critique

RECOMMENDATION

I move that:

1) The Board approve that each Chair prepare its own Operating Plan, and

2) An ADHOC committee be appointed to implement preparation and use of each Chair Operating Plan.

Appendix F
TRAINING SLIDES

MESSAGE TO CHURCH LEADERS
What are your preconceptions?
Do you have capability to change?
Are you open to changes?
Will your preconceptions stand in the way of improving
the efficiency and effectiveness of the church?

Instead of doubting everything that can be doubted, let us
rather doubt nothing until we are compelled to doubt.

CHURCH PROGRAM
MANAGEMENT

POLICY STATEMENT

- IMPLEMENT BETTER RELATIONAL BUSINESS PRACTICE

- INCREASE INVOLVEMENT

- INCREASE VISIBILITY

- DEVELOP WRITTEN PLANS

- MANAGE TO PLANS

PLAN PREPARATION

- WRITTEN PLAN

- WORKING DOCUMENT

- ALL PARTICIPATE IN PREPARATION

- INCREASE VISIBILITY

- INCREASE OWNERSHIP

CURRENT PROBLEMS

- NO WRITTEN PLAN

- REPORTS HAVE NO WRITTEN BASIS

- LITTLE MUTUAL CONTRIBUTION

- MINIMUM INCENTIVE TO IMPROVE

- WORD OF MOUTH CONTINUITY

LEADER INVOLVEMENT

- LEADER/INDIVIDUAL CHAIR MEETINGS

- CHAIR CONTRIBUTES TO EACH CHAIR'S PLAN

TRAINING

- LEADER & CHAIR

- CONGREGATION

RECRUITING COMMITTEE

- ACTIVE YEAR AROUND

- RECRUITS CHAIRS & CHAIR'S STAFF

- MAINTAIN 'ALL-CHURCH' JOB DATABASE

- MAINTAIN CONGREGATION BIOGRAPHIES/RESUMES

STEWARDSHIP COMMITTEE

- ACTIVE THROUGHOUT YEAR

- CONTACT ALL – PLEDGERS & NON-PLEDGERS

- COLLECT CONSTRUCTIVE CRITICISM

BUDGETS & ACCOUNTING

- LAYMAN CHAIR

- ACCOUNTANT

- BUDGET EACH CHAIR

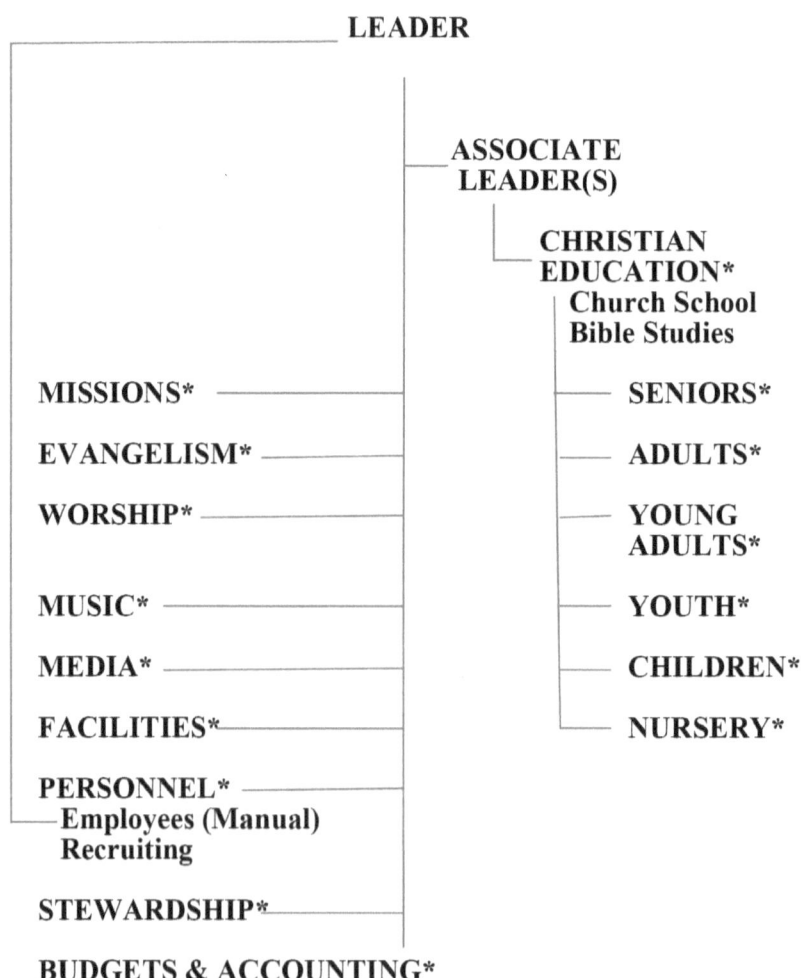

LEADER

ASSOCIATE LEADER(S)

CHRISTIAN EDUCATION*
Church School
Bible Studies

MISSIONS* — **SENIORS***

EVANGELISM* — **ADULTS***

WORSHIP* — **YOUNG ADULTS***

MUSIC* — **YOUTH***

MEDIA* — **CHILDREN***

FACILITIES* — **NURSERY***

PERSONNEL*
Employees (Manual)
Recruiting

STEWARDSHIP*

BUDGETS & ACCOUNTING*

• **Denotes Chairs**

Figure 1 – ORGANIZATIONAL STRUCTURE

GROUP EXERCISE

- CRITIQUE PRESENTED SLIDES

- DEVELOP PLANS

- EXCHANGE PLANS

- CRITIQUE PLANS

Appendix G
CHURCH PROGRAM MANAGEMENT GUIDELINES

MESSAGE TO CHURCH LEADERS
What are your preconceptions?
Do you have capability to change?
Are you open to changes?
Will your preconceptions stand in the way of improving
the efficiency and effectiveness of the church?

Instead of doubting everything that can be doubted, let us
rather doubt nothing until we are compelled to doubt.

POLICY STATEMENT – The Board must pass a POLICY STATEMENT motion that establishes these guidelines as permanent policy. This policy statement should include that the Leader must use these guidelines in conducting <u>EACH</u> Board meeting.

LEADER – The Leader: a) must have <u>interest</u> in program management and at least minimal program management capability in addition to being a biblical scholar who preaches and teaches, and b) must provide direction to each Chair and support the Chair in providing direction to the staff of each Chair.

CHAIR – Each Chair must prepare and implement its own plan and must critique each other Chair's plan.

RECRUITING COMMITTEE – The committee must be active year around and: a) recruit all church positions including Leader, Associate Leader, Chairs, and staff of Chairs, and b) conduct individual training sessions for the Board and congregation.

PLAN – The Leader and each Chair must individually prepare a plan listing tasks to be accomplished and if feasible how the tasks are to be accomplished. Include staffing requirements.

MEETINGS – The Leader must: a) conduct the Board meetings, b) meet with each Chair individually to assist the Chair in plan preparation, and c) discuss status.

BUDGET – Individual budgets must be allocated to the Leader and each Chair.

It should be noted that once the organizational structure is in place, and plans are prepared and each Chair has staffed their component, the organization, the plans, and the staffing can remain in place almost indefinitely. Plans most likely will be revised periodically and staff attrition will require some periodic recruiting.

MEDIA MINISTRIES HISTORY

MESSAGE TO CHURCH LEADERS
What are your preconceptions?
Do you have capability to change?
Are you open to changes?
Will your preconceptions stand in the way of improving
the efficiency and effectiveness of the church?

Instead of doubting everything that can be doubted, let us
rather doubt nothing until we are compelled to doubt.

NOTE: Portions of this Media Ministries operating plan included in **Appendix A** have been redacted to avoid identifying the specific church at which this plan was used. The redacted book location is identified by brackets, thusly, [ ].

Media Ministries was established in memory of [ ] in 2007 and was privately financed and voluntarily managed until January 1, 2015. The tasks performed by Media Ministries include:

- Sound
- Theatrical Lighting
- Video Recording, Processing, and Original Creation
- Computer Projection-Video & Sound
- Assisted Listening
- Still Photography
- DVD Cover Design, Duplication & Distribution
- Audio/Video Mobile Cart
- Support of Church Activities
- Uploading videos of Worship Services, Sermons, Bible Studies, and Special Events to vimeo.com for global access

Twenty-five or more volunteer personnel with desire and capability were recruited at any one time. The video recordings are stored on the website vimeo.com where access to each video was available globally. The global ministry provided videos that were 'completely played' on vimeo.com, not just accessed, in over 120 countries. Examples of the videos are as follows:

Bible Studies:
> World Religions
> Cults
> Ten (10) books of the Bible

Sermons:
> Thirty-nine (39) books of the Bible

Special Events:
> Piano Concerts
> Organ Concerts
> Band Concerts
> Christmas Concerts
> Easter Concerts

Complete Worship Services
> Numerous

It was realized that at some point in time the church would have to assume total responsibility for Media Ministries. So, the church decided to assume responsibility for and manage Media Ministries beginning January 1, 2015. The transition was rough. The global ministry was destroyed by eliminating use of vimeo.com, and the local ministry was significantly limited to: a) supporting worship services, and b) video recording only sermons <u>without</u> <u>editing</u> for uploading to the church website only. Many of the tasks included in the Operating Plan such as lighting, etc. were either eliminated or ignored**. The result of what happened reveals the need to implement significant management changes.**

THE TRANSITION

The author has participated in numerous transitions in for-profit business as well as the church. These transitions were of two types: a) accepting new tasks <u>from</u> others, and b) transferring tasks <u>to</u> others. In all cases there was a mutual understanding and, most of all, acceptance of the tasks as originally defined. In the Media Ministries case, there was little exchange of information. The new leader: a) did not accept the tasks as defined, and b) lacked understanding of tasks as defined. Most of the information available was not transferred because of a lack of interest. Dominant interest became 'sound' with lesser and in some cases no interest in the other tasks. Problems were created by proceeding to make unilateral changes resulting in poor performance. When problems occurred in performing tasks, attempts were made to solve the problems; however, ultimately the tasks were eliminated instead of fixing the problem. Staffing needs were decreased by eliminating tasks, and little effort was spent on recruiting.

Media Ministries was destroyed as a result of poor management, namely 'business as usual' along with use of the relational management technique. This technique allowed Leadership to:
- Have no operating plan
- Provide virtually no direction to participants,
- Have a lack of desire to provide direction,

- Have a lack of desire to participate, thereby limiting their knowledge of the tasks,
- Have a limited understanding and or appreciation of the total scope of the task, and
- Destroy what many churches work so hard to accomplish.

This kind of thing should never be allowed to happen in any organization.

About The Author

Henry Loyd Copeland
BSEE, MS, MBA
Deacon, Elder
Founder: Media Ministries
Author: "Who Is God?"

The author is a Christian lay person with over 40 years of engineering management experience emphasizing the basic functions of management: planning, organizing, staffing, motivating, and controlling. He also taught 'Business' at the Community College level for several years. He recognizes that personnel are one if not the most important ingredient in an organization. As such, he treats personnel with respect. His philosophy is to perform the existing task, and at the same time, spend time and talent to identify new tasks and new ways to perform tasks more efficiently and effectively. He has served as a Deacon and Elder in local churches. He is author of: "Who Is God?". He has had both positive and negative experiences as a member of churches. One negative experience motived him to write this book. This negative experience was the virtual destruction (almost complete non-compliance with the Media Ministries Operating Plan) of Media Ministries; both a local and global ministry that he founded in 2007 and voluntarily financed and managed until January 1, 2015.

About The Book

The purpose of this book is to provide guidelines and motivate churches to more effectively perform the task of managing <u>programs</u> in the church. Management of the church, the BODY OF CHRIST on earth, is a very serious matter. As such, the church should be most interested in improving its efficiency and effectiveness. However, without knowing, many church Leaders continue to make no major changes in their management philosophy. In other words, 'business as usual' prevails.

Each church leader who reads this book must pay close attention to terms as defined in this book. It is recognized that churches have different organizational structures and identify different tasks and manage their church programs differently. This book presents a more classical management approach that is more consistent with secular business/management textbooks. This approach is widely used in business and is essential to success of the business. This approach can be a little foreign to those who have not used this approach. For example, the reader can be strongly inclined to say: "We don't do it this way." Yes, the reader must read the book as <u>a learning process</u> and understand what is being said even though it might be 'foreign' at first.

It is recognized that members of the church are from all ages and from different backgrounds. These differences result in the need for churches to adapt accordingly. However, all churches regardless of their outward operation must utilize the basic functions of management. For example, organizational components of the church must identify exactly what tasks they are to perform. This list of tasks comprises a plan. Experience shows that there are many advantages of preparing written plans. The same kinds of comments as stated here also apply to organizing, staffing, motivating, and controlling.

Free Preview

The entire organization shown in Figure 1 – ORGANIZATIONAL STRUCTURE is referred to in this book as the "Leadership Board" and Board will be used for short. The Board in some churches is called Board of Deacons, and the Board in other churches is called Session. Other churches might have different names for the Board. The Board is composed of Components which are **top level** areas of responsibility. This terminology is not intended to represent any one or more religious traditions. This terminology is unique to this book. The Leader is in charge of the Board and a Chair is in charge of a Component. *The Board as a whole is not considered the Leader in this book. There is only one Leader who is the Leader of the Board and this Leader is responsible for the performance of each Chair. This Leader provides guidance and direction to each Chair.* The Leader's job description should include both management and spiritual. The Leader is a salaried professional ordained minister and has line authority over the Associate Leaders and the Chairs. Associate Leaders are salaried professionals who have expertise in one or more church discipline and a) perform their tasks within that discipline which is within the scope of one or more Components, and b) advise Chairs. The Chairs are volunteer members of the church and have authority over Associate Leaders. Each Chair should have its own task and its own budget to accomplish the task. For example, one Chair should <u>not</u> have control of all or part of the budget of another Chair. The Budgets & Accounting Chair should have final approval of the entire budget. Each Chair has to assume responsibility for <u>contributing</u> to the success not only of a Component but also for the success of the entire Board by providing guidance or constructive criticism of each other Chair's plan and performance to plan. **Appendix C** Example of Chair Critique- There will be cases where one or more tasks will be common to more than one Chair. An example of this task is shown in **Appendix B** – Hosting. Unless the Board assumes such responsibility, it is possible that any one or more of its Components could perform poorly and even become totally ineffective.

Implementation of the guidelines in this book will occur slowly and leadership must be **dedicated** and **persistent**. Leadership also will need to do a lot of **training.** Patience is required as well as continued FOLLOW THROUGH. Satisfactory results will be forthcoming.

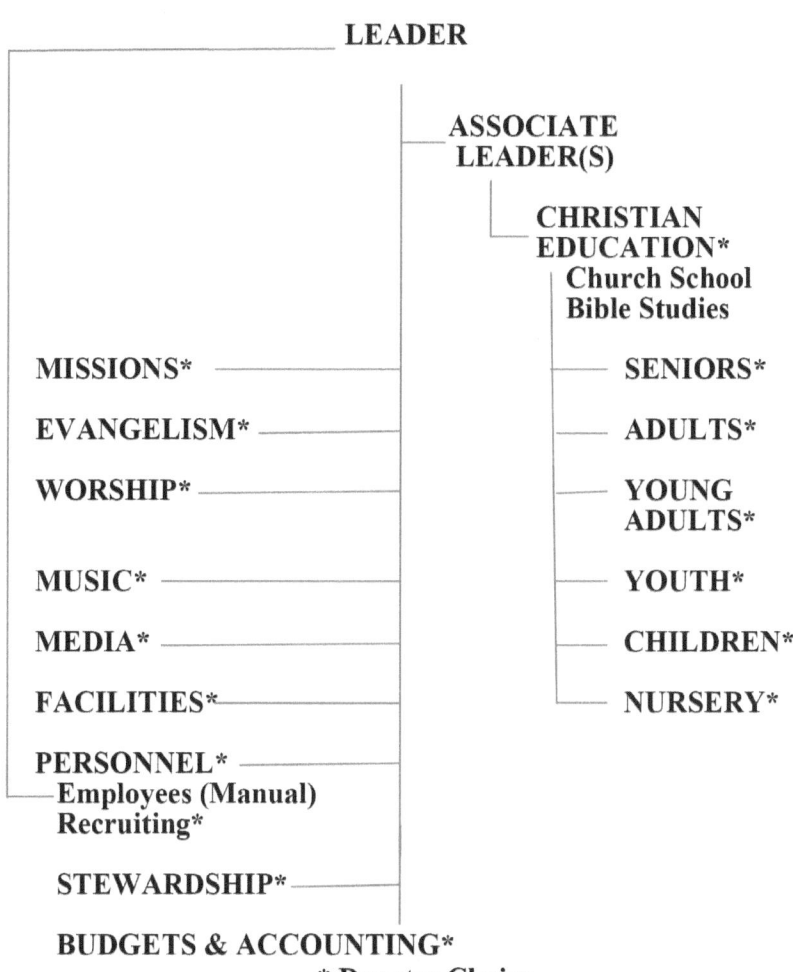

Figure 1 – ORGANIZATIONAL STRUCTURE

Keynote

Guidelines are provided to identify and manage
church programs efficiently and effectively.

www.ingramcontent.com/pod-product-compliance
Lightning Source LLC
Chambersburg PA
CBHW030905180526
45163CB00004B/1718